PRIMARY MATHEMATICS 1A

TEXTBOOK

Marshall Cavendish
Education

SingaporeMath.com Inc®

Original edition published under the title Primary Mathematics Textbook 1A

© 1981 Curriculum Planning & Development Division

Ministry of Education, Singapore

Published by Times Media Private Limited

This American Edition

© 2003 Times Media Private Limited

© 2003 Marshall Cavendish International (Singapore) Private Limited

Published by Marshall Cavendish Education

An imprint of Marshall Cavendish International (Singapore) Private Limited

Times Centre, 1 New Industrial Road, Singapore 536196

Customer Service Hotline: (65) 6411 0820

E-mail: tmesales@sg.marshallcavendish.com

Website: www.marshallcavendish.com/education

SingaporeMath.com Inc®

Distributed by

SingaporeMath.com Inc

404 Beavercreek Road #225

Oregon City, OR 97045

U.S.A.

Website: www.singaporemath.com

First published 2003

Second impression 2003

Reprinted 2004

Third impression 2004

Fourth impression 2005

Reprinted 2005, 2006 (twice), 2007, 2008, 2009 (twice),
        2010, 2011 (twice)

ISBN 978-981-01-8494-0

Printed in Malaysia by Times Offset (M) Sdn Bhd

ACKNOWLEDGEMENTS

Our special thanks to Richard Askey, Professor of Mathematics (University of Wisconsin, Madison), Yoram Sagher, Professor of Mathematics (University of Illinois, Chicago), and Madge Goldman, President (Gabriella and Paul Rosenbaum Foundation), for their indispensable advice and suggestions in the production of Primary Mathematics (U.S. Edition).

PREFACE

Primary Mathematics (U.S. Edition) comprises textbooks and workbooks. The main feature of this package is the use of the **Concrete** ➡ **Pictorial** ➡ **Abstract** approach. The students are provided with the necessary learning experiences beginning with the concrete and pictorial stages, followed by the abstract stage to enable them to learn mathematics meaningfully. This package encourages active thinking processes, communication of mathematical ideas and problem solving.

The textbook comprises 9 units. Each unit is divided into parts: ❶, ❷, . . . Each part starts with a meaningful situation for communication and is followed by specific learning tasks numbered 1, 2, . . . The textbook is accompanied by a workbook. The sign ⌐Workbook Exercise⟩ is used to link the textbook to the workbook exercises.

Practice exercises are designed to provide the students with further practice after they have done the relevant workbook exercises. Review exercises are provided for cumulative reviews of concepts and skills. All the practice exercises and review exercises are optional exercises.

The color patch ▇ is used to invite active participation from the students and to facilitate oral discussion. The students are advised not to write on the color patches.

CONTENTS

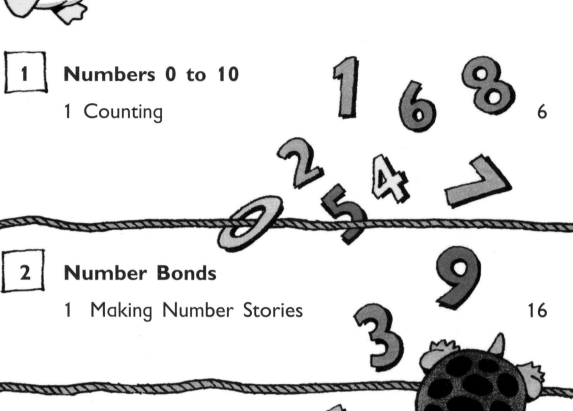

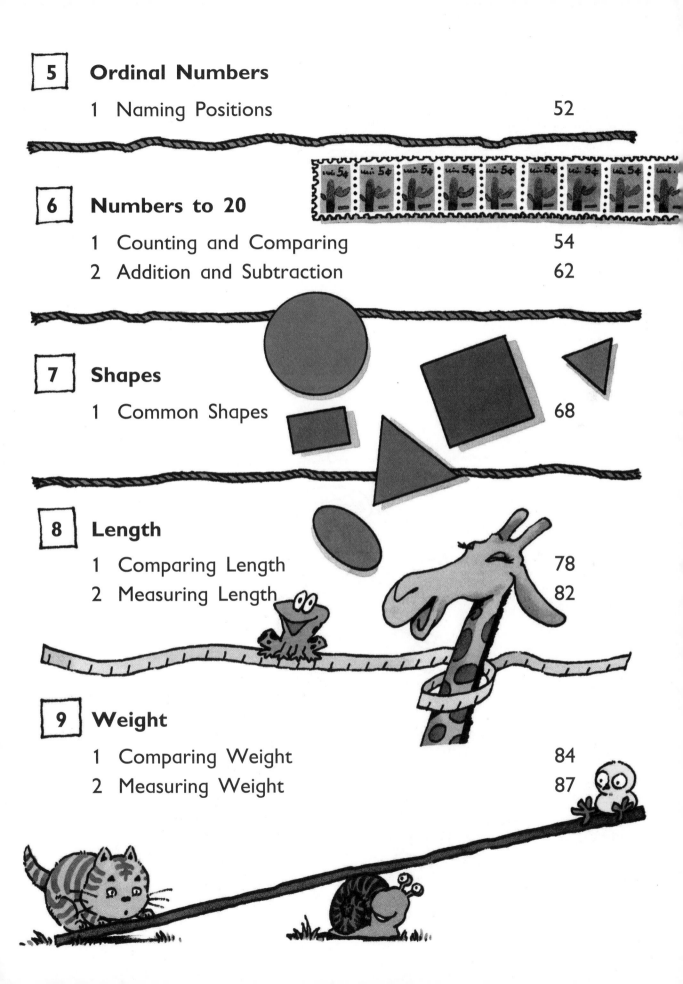

Numbers 0 to 10

1 Counting

0
zero

1
one

2
two

3

three

4

four

5

five

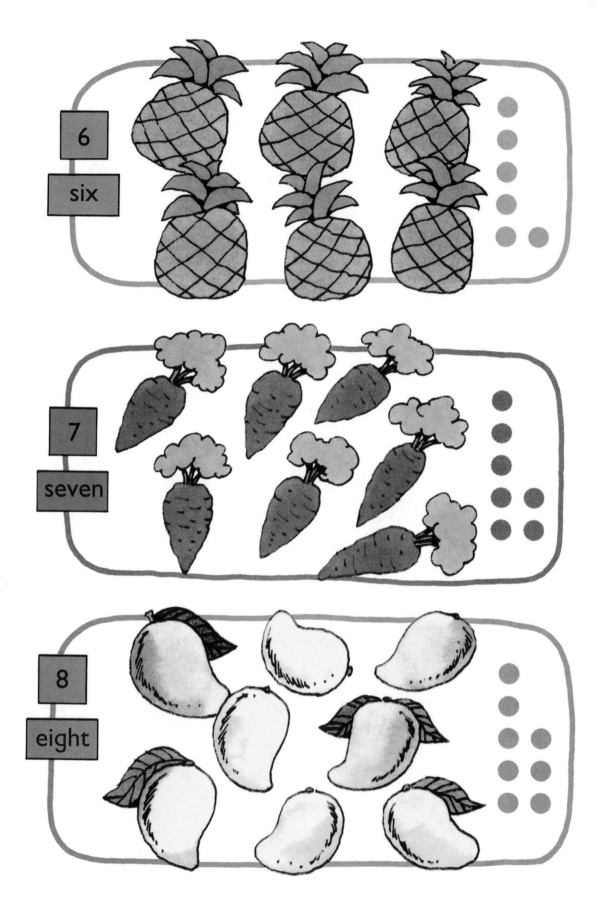

6
six

7
seven

8
eight

9
nine

10
ten

1. Let's count.

11

2. Do the sets have the same number?

(a)

(b)

(c)

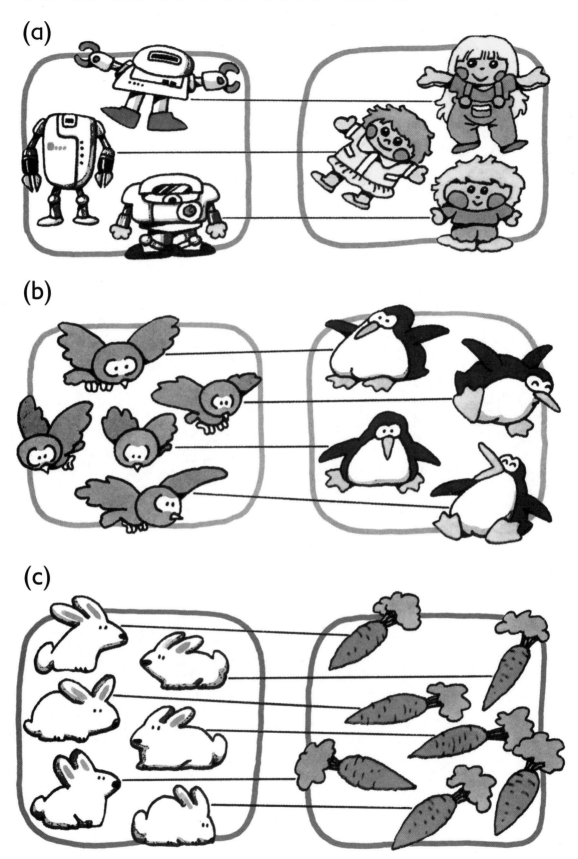

3. How many butterflies are there?

4. Which set has **more**?

5. Which set has **less**?

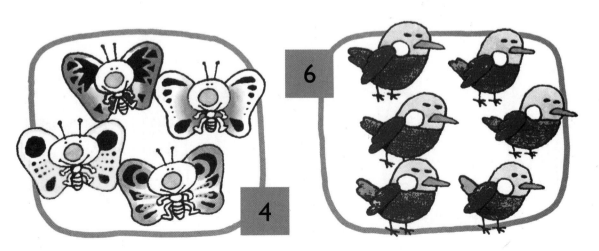

6. Count from 1 to 10.

7. What comes next?

8. What comes next?

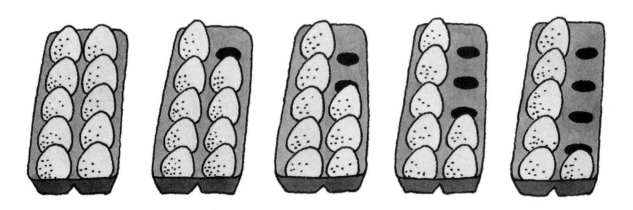

9. Count backwards.

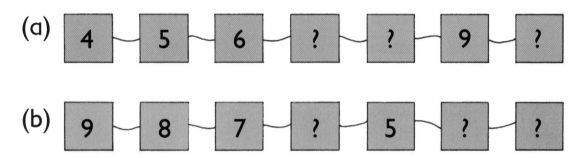

10. What are the missing numbers?

(a)

| 4 | 5 | 6 | ? | ? | 9 | ? |

(b)

| 9 | 8 | 7 | ? | 5 | ? | ? |

(c)

Number Bonds

1 Making Number Stories

There are 5 penguins.
2 are swimming.
3 are not swimming.

16

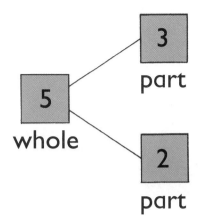

3
part

5
whole

2
part

Make up other stories of 5 about the penguins.

5

2

3

5

4

1

1. **Make up as many stories as you can about the 6 children.**

2. **Find other pairs of numbers that make 6.**

1 and 5 make 6.

3. Make up as many stories as you can about the 7 balloons.

4. Find other pairs of numbers that make 7.

3 and 4 make 7.

5. (a) Make up a story of 8 from the picture.

(b) Tell other stories of 8.

6. Find other pairs of numbers that make 8.

4 and 4 make 8.

8 — 4
   — 4

4   4   2   6

0   5   3

8   1   7

Workbook Exercise 7

7. Find other pairs of numbers that make 9.

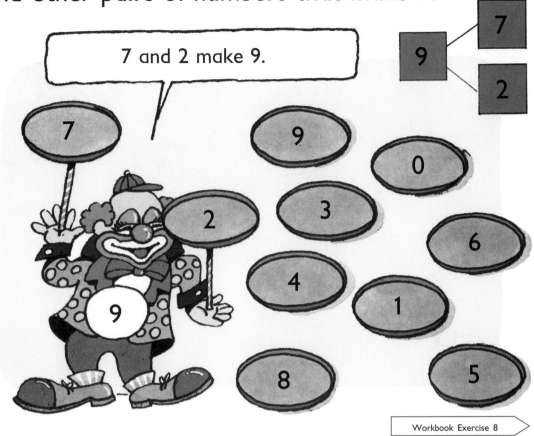

7 and 2 make 9.

Workbook Exercise 8

8. Find other pairs of numbers that make 10.

4 and 6 make 10.

Workbook Exercise 9

9. What are the missing numbers?

(a)

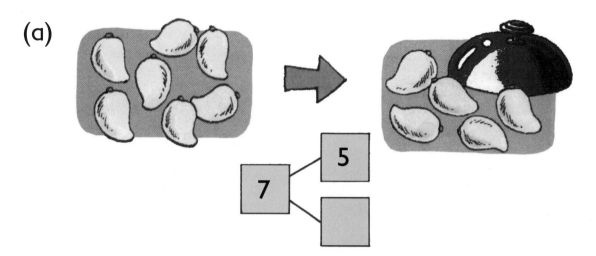

(b)

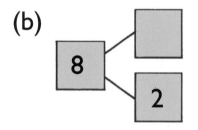

(c)

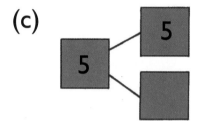

(d)

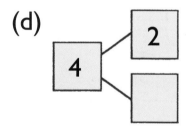

(e)

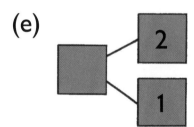

(f)

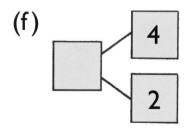

(g)

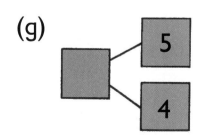

Workbook Exercise 10

10.

6 and ⬛ make 10.

11. Play with a friend.

Make two sets of cards numbered 0 to 10:

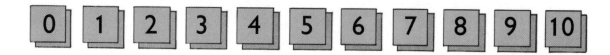

0 1 2 3 4 5 6 7 8 9 10

Use the cards to make as many tens as you can.

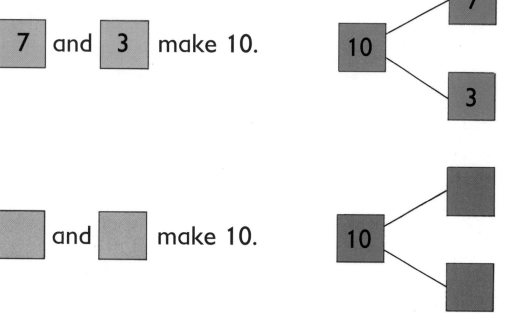

7 and 3 make 10.

10 — 7
10 — 3

⬛ and ⬛ make 10.

10 — ⬛
10 — ⬛

23

3 Addition

1 Making Addition Stories

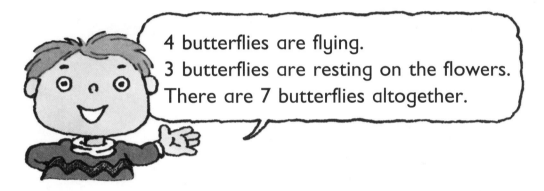

4 butterflies are flying.
3 butterflies are resting on the flowers.
There are 7 butterflies altogether.

We write the number sentence:

4 + 3 = 7

This is **addition**.
It means **putting together**.

Add 4 and 3.
The answer is 7.

4 + 3 = 7

There are 6 red flowers.
There are 4 yellow flowers.
There are 10 flowers altogether.

6 + 4 = 10

3 children are playing.
2 more are coming.
There are 5 children altogether.

3 + 2 = 5

1. Make up a story for each number sentence.

(a)

$$2 + 4 = 6$$

(b)

$$5 + 4 = 9$$

(c)

3 + 2 = 5

(d)

3 + 0 = 3

2. Make up as many stories as you can for each number sentence.

$$4 + 2 = 6$$
$$3 + 3 = 6$$

3. Make up as many **addition** stories as you can. Write a number sentence for each story.

Workbook Exercises 12 to 14

2 Addition With Number Bonds

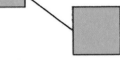

6 + 2 = [ ]

2 + 6 = [ ]

5 + 3 = [ ]

3 + 5 = [ ]

4 + 4 = [ ]

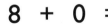

7 + 1 = [ ]

1 + 7 = [ ]

8 + 0 = [ ]

0 + 8 = [ ]

1.

How many birds are there altogether?

6 + 2 =

There are ☐ birds altogether.

2.

How many robots do they have altogether?

4 + 3 =

They have ☐ robots altogether.

3. Complete the number sentences.

(a)

3 + 3 =

(b)

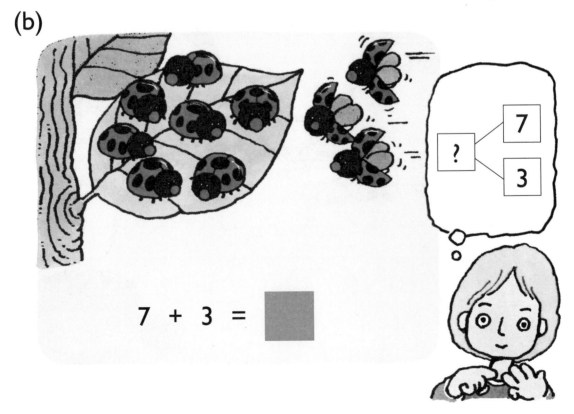

7 + 3 =

3 Other Methods of Addition

4 + 1 = ☐

4 + 2 = ☐

4 + 3 = ☐

33

1. Add 6 and 1.

Begin with 6 and count on: (7)

6 + 1 =

2. Add 7 and 2.

Begin with 7 and count on: (8), (9)

7 + 2 =

3. Add 4 and 3.

Count on from 4:
⑤, ⑥, ⑦

4 + 3 = ☐

4. Complete the addition sentences.

(a) 4 + 0 = ☐

5 + 0 = ☐

8 + 0 = ☐

(b) 5 + 1 = ☐

7 + 1 = ☐

9 + 1 = ☐

(c) 3 + 2 = ☐

6 + 2 = ☐

8 + 2 = ☐

(d) 5 + 3 = ☐

6 + 3 = ☐

7 + 3 = ☐

35

Workbook Exercise 18

5. Complete the addition sentences.

(a)

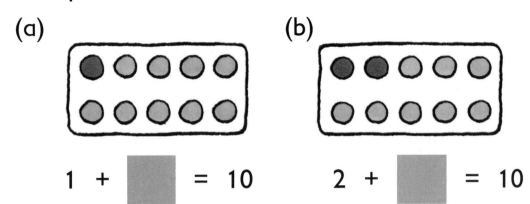

1 + ☐ = 10

(b)

2 + ☐ = 10

(c)

3 + ☐ = 10

(d)

4 + ☐ = 10

(e) 5 + ☐ = 10

(f) 6 + ☐ = 10

(g) 7 + ☐ = 10

(h) 8 + ☐ = 10

(i) 9 + ☐ = 10

(j) 10 + ☐ = 10

6. Which rats will each cat catch?

4

Subtraction

1 Making Subtraction Stories

There are 8 birds.
3 birds fly away.
5 birds are left.

We write the number sentence:

$$8 - 3 = 5$$

This is **subtraction**.
It means **taking away**.

Subtract 3 from 8.
The answer is 5.

8 – 3 = 5

$$7 - 2 = 5$$

There are 7 children.
2 of them are girls.
There are 5 boys.

There are 9 carrots altogether.
The rabbits are eating 3 carrots.
6 carrots are left.

$$9 - 3 = 6$$

1. Make up a story for each number sentence.

(a)

$5 - 1 = 4$

(b)

$9 - 3 = 6$

(c)

$6 - 4 = 2$

(d)

$6 - 6 = 0$

2. Make up as many stories as you can for each number sentence.

$$7 - 3 = 4$$
$$7 - 2 = 5$$

3. Make up as many **subtraction** stories as you can. Write a number sentence for each story.

43

② Methods of Subtraction

6 – 2 = ☐

6 – 4 = ☐

6 – 1 = ☐

6 – 5 = ☐

6

6 – 3 = ☐

6 – 6 = ☐

6 – 0 = ☐

1.

How many balloons are left?

6 − 2 = ▢

▢ balloons are left.

2.

Emily

Morgan

5 dolls belong to Morgan.
The rest belong to Emily.
How many dolls does Emily have?

8 − 5 = ▢

Emily has ▢ dolls.

3.   Complete the number sentences.

(a)

$$8 - 2 = \boxed{}$$

(b)

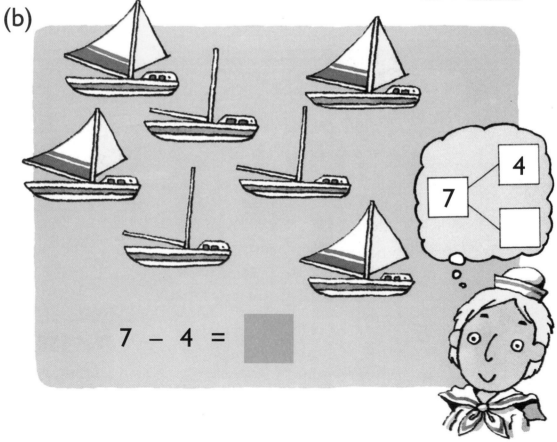

$$7 - 4 = \boxed{}$$

Workbook Exercises 23 & 24

4. Complete the number sentences.

(a)

3 + 2 = ☐   5 − 2 = ☐

2 + 3 = ☐   5 − 3 = ☐

(b)

7 + 2 = ☐   9 − 2 = ☐

2 + 7 = ☐   9 − 7 = ☐

Workbook Exercises 25 & 26

5. Subtract 1 from 5.

Begin with 5 and count backwards: (4)

5 − 1 =

6. Subtract 2 from 7.

Begin with 7 and count backwards: (6), (5)

7 − 2 =

7. Subtract 3 from 10.

Count backwards from 10: ⑨, ⑧, ⑦

10 − 3 = ▢

8. Complete the subtraction sentences.

(a) 3 − 0 = ▢

5 − 0 = ▢

8 − 0 = ▢

(b) 4 − 1 = ▢

7 − 1 = ▢

9 − 1 = ▢

(c) 5 − 2 = ▢

6 − 2 = ▢

10 − 2 = ▢

(d) 5 − 3 = ▢

8 − 3 = ▢

9 − 3 = ▢

Workbook Exercise 27

9. Complete the subtraction sentences.

(a) 5 − 5 = ☐

5 − 4 = ☐

5 − 3 = ☐

(b) 9 − 9 = ☐

9 − 8 = ☐

9 − 7 = ☐

(c) 3 − 2 = ☐

6 − 5 = ☐

9 − 8 = ☐

(d) 6 − 4 = ☐

7 − 5 = ☐

8 − 6 = ☐

10. Subtract 6 from 10.

6 and 4 make 10.

10 − 6 = ☐

11. Complete the subtraction sentences.

(a) 10 − 3 = ☐

(b) 10 − 5 = ☐

(c) 10 − 8 = ☐

(d) 10 − 9 = ☐

50

12. Which train does each car belong to?

Workbook Exercises 29 to 31

Ordinal Numbers

1 **Naming Positions**

Who comes in first?

| 1st | 2nd | 3rd | 4th | 5th | 6th |
| first | second | third | fourth | fifth | sixth |

52

1.

the 5th position

5 children

Who is 5th?

Who is 9th?

In which position is the boy E?

Workbook Exercises 32 & 33

2.

left

right

 is 3rd from the **left**.

 is 2nd from the **right**.

Who is 4th from the left?

Who is 6th from the right?

Workbook Exercise 34

6 Numbers to 20

1 Counting and Comparing

Count all the eggs:
1, 2, 3, 4, 5, 6, 7, 8,
9, 10, 11, 12, 13

11	12	13	14	15
eleven	twelve	thirteen	fourteen	fifteen

Count on from 10: 11, 12, 13.

13 is 10 and 3.

16 sixteen

17 seventeen

18 eighteen

19 nineteen

20 twenty

1. Make a ten and count.

(a)

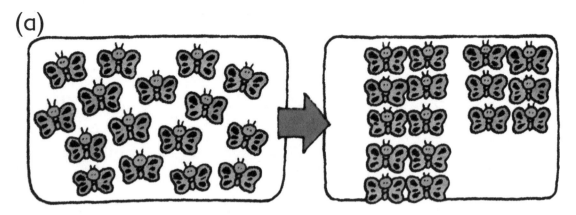

[   ] is 10 and 6.

(b)

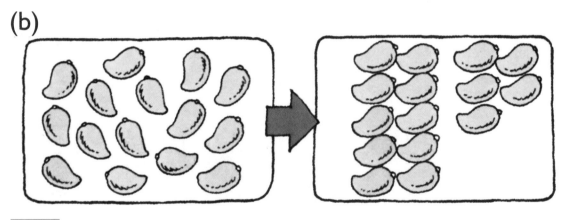

[   ] is 10 and 5.

(c)

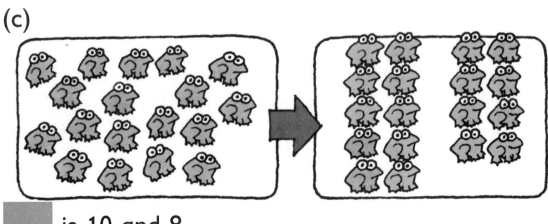

[   ] is 10 and 8.

2. (a) How many beads are there?

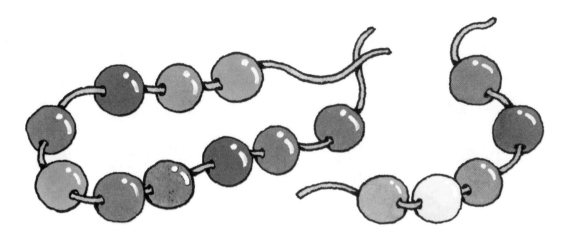

(b) 10 and 5 make .

(c) 10 + 5 =

3. (a) How many stamps are there?

(b) 10 and 4 make .

(c) 10 + 4 =

4. Complete the addition sentences.

(a)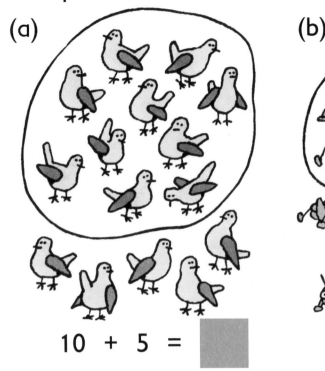

10 + 5 = ☐

(b)

10 + ☐ = ☐

Workbook Exercise 37

5. Count from 1 to 20.

Then count backwards.

20, 19, 18, ...

6. What are the missing numbers?

(a)

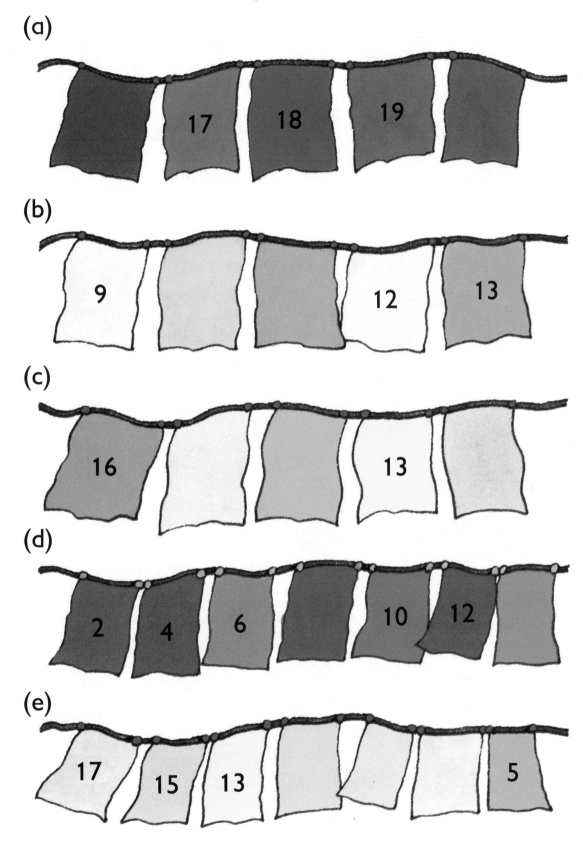

17   18   19

(b)

9   12   13

(c)

16   13

(d)

2   4   6   10   12

(e)

17   15   13   5

7. Which set has the **greater** number?

A B

8. Which set has the **smaller** number?

A B

9. Which set has the **greatest** number?
Which set has the **smallest** number?

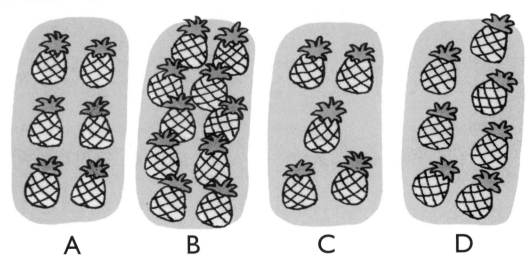

A B C D

10. (a) Which is greater, 14 or 17?

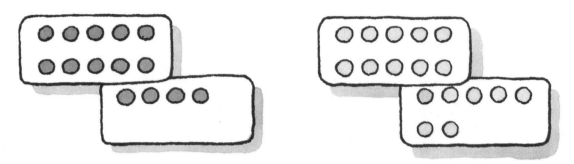

(b) Which is smaller, 19 or 12?

11. Compare these numbers:

(a) Which number is the greatest?

(b) Which number is the smallest?

(c) Arrange the numbers in order. Begin with the smallest.

Workbook Exercise 39

2 Addition and Subtraction

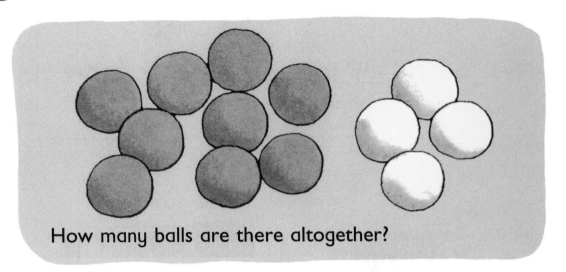

How many balls are there altogether?

Make 10 first.

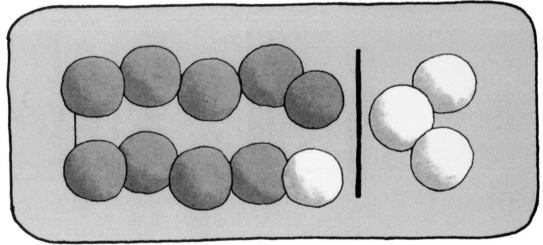

9 + 4 =

There are ☐ balls altogether.

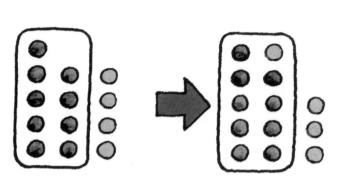

9 and 1 make 10.

10 + 3 = 13

1. **Add by making 10 first.**

(a)

5 + 9 = ▢

(b)

7 + 8 =

$$7 + 8$$
$$\diagdown \diagup$$
$$5 \quad 2$$

2. Complete the addition sentences.

(a) 9 + 1 =   9 + 8 =

(b) 8 + 2 =   8 + 6 =

(c) 1 + 9 =   3 + 9 =

(d) 2 + 8 =   5 + 8 =

(e) 3 + 7 =   6 + 7 =

Workbook Exercises 40 & 41

3. Add 13 and 4.

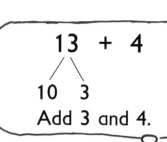

13 + 4
/\
10 3
Add 3 and 4.

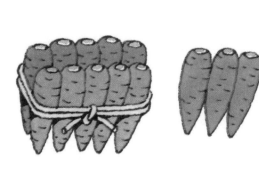

13 + 4 =

4. Complete the addition sentences.

(a) 5 + 4 = 9

15 + 4 =

5 + 14 =

(b) 2 + 8 = 10

12 + 8 =

2 + 18 =

Workbook Exercise 42

5. Subtract 4 from 16.

16 – 4
/\
10 6
Subtract 4 from 6.

16 – 4 =

6. Complete the subtraction sentences.

(a) 8 – 3 = 5

18 – 3 = ▢

(b) 7 – 5 = 2

17 – 5 = ▢

Workbook Exercise 43

7. Subtract 4 from 12.

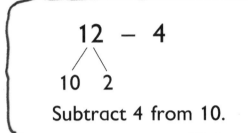

12 – 4

10   2

Subtract 4 from 10.

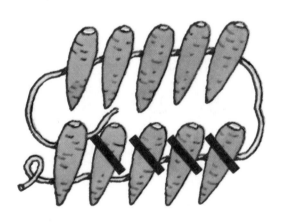

12 – 4 = ▢

8. Complete the subtraction sentences.

(a) 10 – 6 = 4

11 – 6 = ▢

12 – 6 = ▢

15 – 6 = ▢

(b) 10 – 7 = 3

11 – 7 = ▢

12 – 7 = ▢

15 – 7 = ▢

Workbook Exercise 44

9. Add 8 and 3.

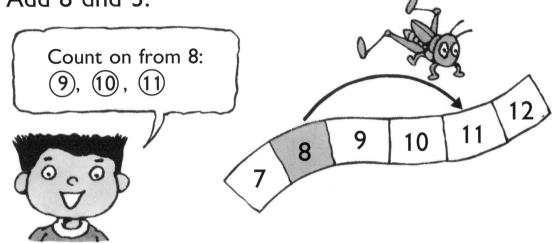

Count on from 8:
⑨, ⑩, ⑪

10. Complete the addition sentences.

(a) 9 + 2 = ▢   (b) 9 + 3 = ▢

(c) 15 + 1 = ▢   (d) 17 + 2 = ▢

11. Subtract 2 from 11.

Count backwards from 11:
⑩, ⑨

12. Complete the subtraction sentences.

(a) 11 − 3 = ▢   (b) 12 − 3 = ▢

(c) 14 − 1 = ▢   (d) 18 − 2 = ▢

Workbook Exercises 45 to 49

7

Shapes

·············

1 Common Shapes

1. Compare the objects in each set with the given shape.

(a)

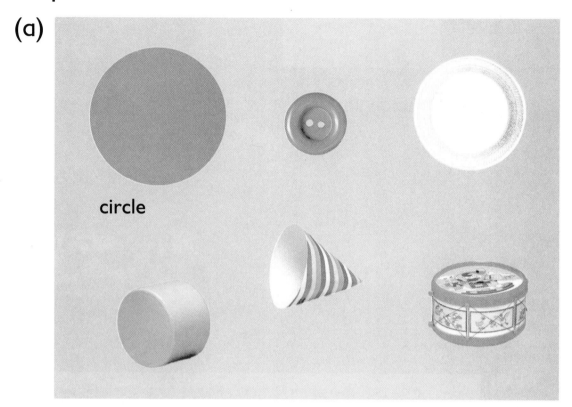

circle

(b)

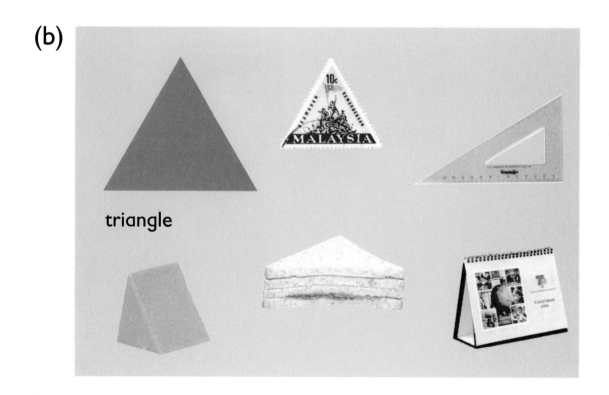

triangle

(c)

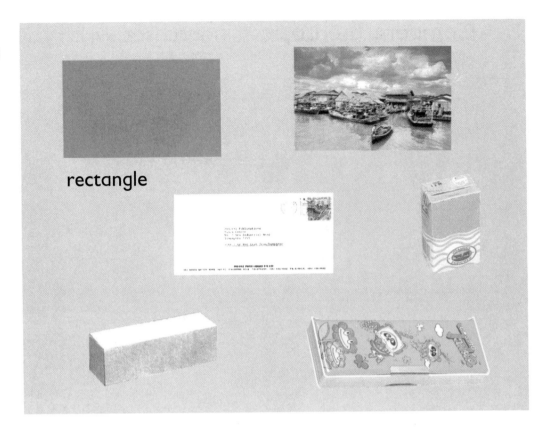

rectangle

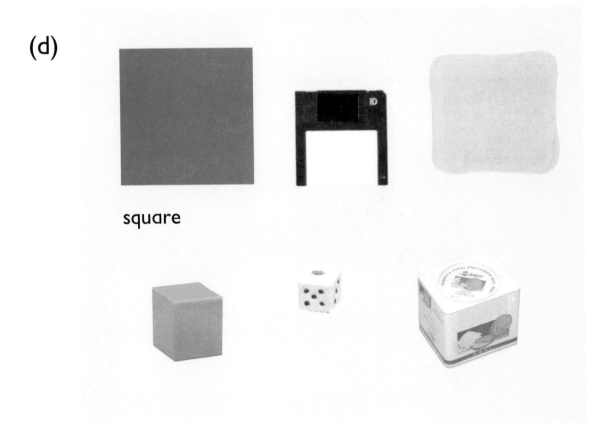

(d)

square

2. Group these shapes in different ways.

(a)

I group them by shape: circles, squares, triangles and rectangles.

Which group does each of these belong to?

(b)

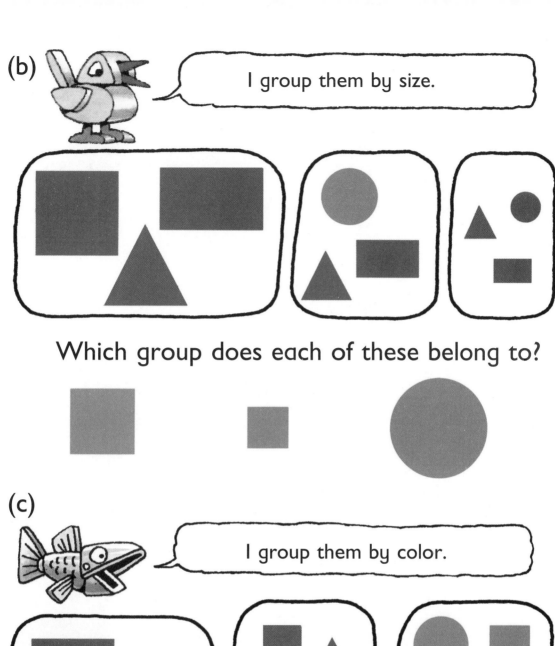

I group them by size.

Which group does each of these belong to?

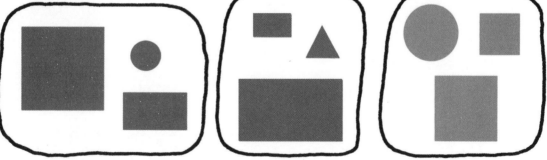

(c)

I group them by color.

Which group does each of these belong to?

Workbook Exercises 52 & 53

3. Are the holes of the same shape?
   Are they of the same size?

(a)

(b)

(c)

(d)

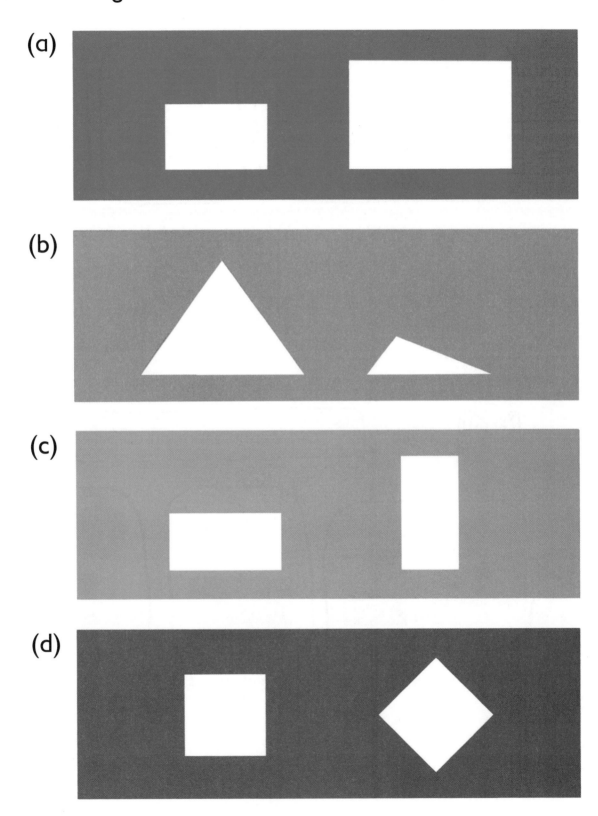

4. These are patterns of shapes.
What comes next in each pattern?

(a)

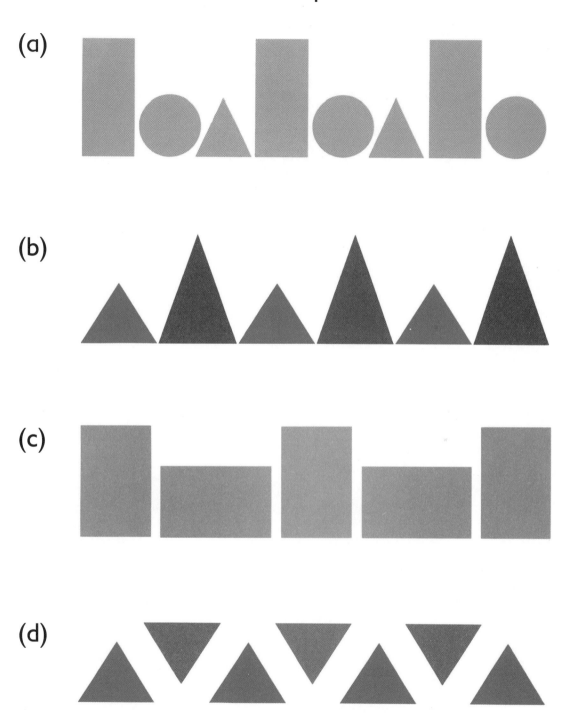

(b)

(c)

(d)

75

Workbook Exercise 54

5. Pair up these pieces to form 3 circles.

6. Pair up these pieces to form a square and a triangle.

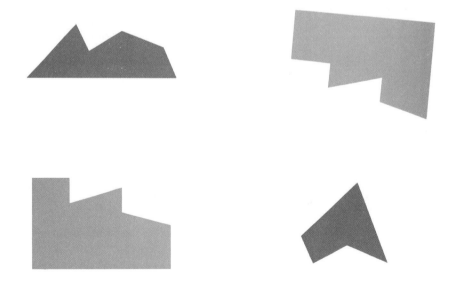

7. We can fit these 4 pieces together to form a shape.

Here is an example:

Trace the 4 pieces on a piece of paper and cut them out.
Use the 4 pieces to form each of these shapes.

(a)

(b)

77

8 Length

1 Comparing Length

I am **longer** than Miss Caterpillar.

I am **shorter** than Mr. Snake.

Am I the **shortest?**

Who is the **longest?**

Who is the **shortest?**

I am **taller** than Mr. Elephant.

I am **shorter** than Miss Giraffe.

Am I the **shortest?**

Who is the **tallest?**

Who is the **shortest?**

1. Which is the longest string?
   Which is the shortest string?

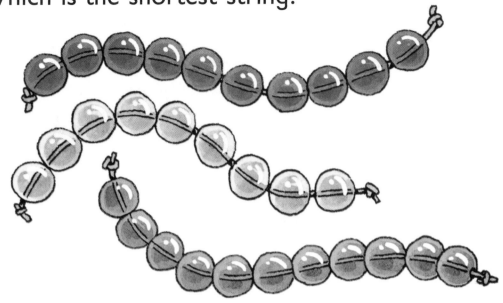

2. Which is the tallest block?
   Which is the shortest block?

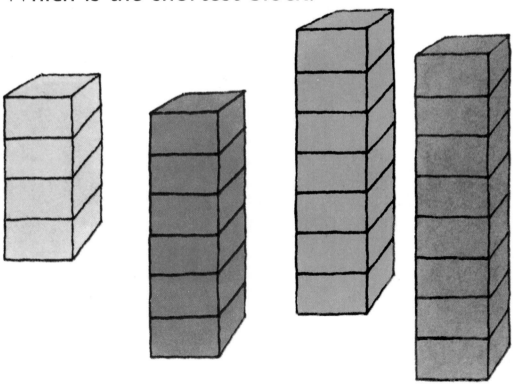

3.

Which worm takes the longest path?

Which worm takes the shortest path?

4.

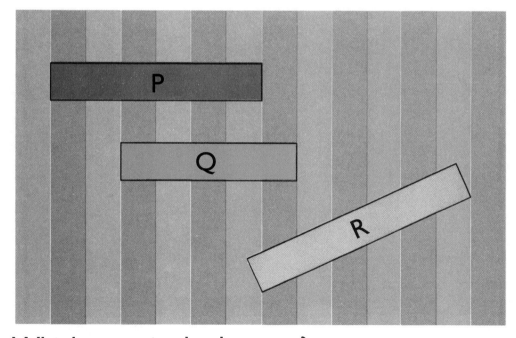

Which tape is the longest?

Which tape is the shortest?

Workbook Exercises 56 & 57

2 Measuring Length

John uses ice-cream sticks to measure the length of a table.

Each ice-cream stick stands for 1 unit.

The length of the table is about **12** units.

1. Mary uses paper-clips as units to measure the length of a book.

The length of the book is about units.

2. Make a chain of 20 paper clips like this:

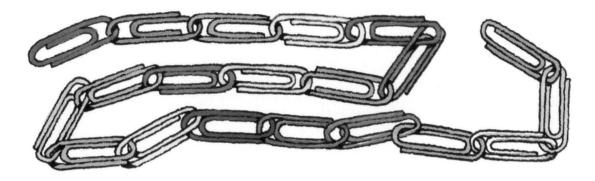

(a) The length of the chain is units.

(b) Use the chain to measure your hand and your foot.

 My hand is about units long.

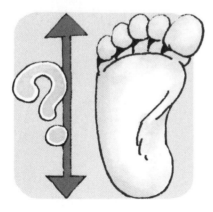 My foot is about units long.

(c) Which is longer, your hand or your foot?

Weight

1 **Comparing Weight**

The cupboard is **heavier** than the chair.

The chair is **lighter** than the cupboard.

Which is the **lightest**?

Which is the **heaviest**?

The mango is **as heavy as** the ball.

The orange is **lighter** than the ball.

The ball is **heavier** than the orange.

1. Which weighs more?

   (a)

   (b)

2. How many marbles balance the block?

3.

The clay ball is as heavy as the book.

Make a clay ball as heavy as your ruler.

2 Measuring Weight

Matthew uses clothes-pins to measure the weight of a pair of scissors.

Each clothes-pin stands for 1 unit.

The weight of the scissors is ☐ units.

Then he uses marbles to measure the weight of the same pair of scissors.

Each marble stands for 1 unit.

The weight of the scissors is ☐ units.

1.

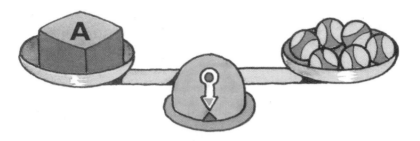

Box A weighs ☐ units.

Box B weighs ☐ units.

Box C weighs ☐ units.

Which box is the heaviest?

Which box is the lighest?

2. Find out how many marbles balance your pencil box.